TWIGS & KNUCKLEBONES

BOOKS BY SARAH LINDSAY

POETRY

Twigs and Knucklebones
Mount Clutter
Primate Behavior

CHAPBOOKS

Insomniac's Lullaby
Bodies of Water

TWIGS & KNUCKLEBONES

Sarah Lindsay

Copper Canyon Press
Port Townsend, Washington

Printed in the United States of America

Cover art: Mark Calderon, *Stemma*, 1990. Tea, blood, cement and steel, 25 × 13 × 1.5 inches. Courtesy of Greg Kucera Gallery, Seattle.

Copper Canyon Press is in residence at Fort Worden State Park in Port Townsend, Washington, under the auspices of Centrum. Centrum is a gathering place for artists and creative thinkers from around the world, students of all ages and backgrounds, and audiences seeking extraordinary cultural enrichment.

LIBRARY OF CONGRESS CATALOGING-IN-PUBLICATION DATA

Lindsay, Sarah, 1958–
Twigs and knucklebones / Sarah Lindsay.
  p. cm.
ISBN 978-1-55659-164-8 (pbk.: alk. paper)
I. Title.
PS3562.I51192T85 2008
811'.54—dc22

2008019578

98765432 FIRST PRINTING

COPPER CANYON PRESS
Post Office Box 271
Port Townsend, Washington 98368

www.coppercanyonpress.org

To Mary K., Allan, and Gertrude,
mit Schlag

ACKNOWLEDGMENTS

The author thanks Michael Wiegers, Copper Canyon Press, and copy editor David Caligiuri; she also wishes to thank George Bradley and Kay Ryan for help and mental nourishment; John Balaban for crucial facilitation; Herb Leibowitz for asking—twice—about sending photos; Brad Leithauser for travel real and imagined; David Rigsbee and Mount Olive College for the pickles; Joan Bingham for encouragement; Red and Patti Jo Watson for stirring up neurons; Isabel and Jonathan Zuber for careful reading; Mark Smith-Soto and Valerie Nieman for help with poems Past and Yet to Come; three nieces for fun in Hawaii and the line "I love you more than fish"; Phyllis Lindsay for playing on plumbing; Allan Troxler for the zucchini shofar and Easter Bunnyhood; Lisa and S'mizz for computer ed. and comic relief; Sir Leonard Woolley, Sir Flinders Petrie, and Sir Douglas Mawson for general magnificence; and Pace, the Sky people, and Holy Moley! Coley PR for invaluable support. She wishes to salute the Admiral and dedicate this book to Mary K., Allan, and Gertrude, mit Schlag.

Grateful acknowledgment is made to the following publications, in which these poems first appeared: *Cave Wall:* "From the Elephants' Graveyard," "Loving a Saint"; *Experience: Centrum's Magazine for the Creative Life:* "More Than Water"; *The Greensboro Review:* "Real Live Boy," "Scapegoat of Eske's Field"; *International Poetry Review:* "Look Again," "Underground Orchids," "Vulture Feather"; *Mantis: A Journal of Poetry and Translation:* "The Ruins of Nab"; *Narrative Magazine:* "Song of a Spadefoot Toad"; *The National Poetry Review:* "From the Files of a Recording Angel"; *Notre Dame Review:* "Beyond Rubies," "Destruction," "The Invention of Comfort"; *Orion:* "Starlings on the Line"; *Parnassus: Poetry in Review:* "Valhalla Burn Unit on the Moon Callisto" (reprinted in *McSweeney's*), "Flukes," "The Blessed Elias and the Worm"; *The Pedestal Magazine* (www .thepedestalmagazine.com): "Land's End"; *Poetry:* "Elegy for the Quagga," "Makris Is Fallen," "Small Moth," "The So-called Singer of Nab," "Stubbornly," "Tell the Bees," "Unreliable Narration," and "Zucchini Shofar"; and to *From the Fishouse* (www .fishousepoems.org) for its audio files on the Web of the author reading "Look Again," "Valhalla Burn Unit on the Moon Callisto," and "Underground Orchids."

Contents

TWIGS & KNUCKLEBONES

PART I

Flukes

Song of a Spadefoot Toad

We stand by the patch of grass marked his.
But he is no longer subject
to the whims of this bewildering sphere,
with its sound waves, cancers, specific gravity, spring,
where we still live, where ostrich chicks
before hatching sing through the eggshell,
where filarial worms in bloodstream darkness
know when it's night, and drift to the skin
of their host, so mosquitoes
will drink them and bear them away.

Did he look without eyes
once more as if over his shoulder,
did his old home shrink
to a rolling marble?—
where elephants hollow out caves in a mountain
to eat its salt, where ants shelter aphids
and drink their sweet green milk,
where a black-tailed prairie dog bolts
through a tunnel with an infant head
and scarlet neck in its mouth.

We who still recoil from death,
how can we picture where he is now?—
when we labor to comprehend
this place, where minute crustaceans
pierce the side of a swordfish
to lodge in its heart, where spadefoot toads
wake from eleven months' sleep and sing
till their throats bleed, where humans
do everything humans do, where a fig wasp

pollinates a flower while laying her eggs,
then lies on her side as baby nematodes
crawl from her half-eaten gut, and where faithfully
every day in mangrove shallows
paired seahorses—armless, legless, without expression—
dance with each other at sunrise.

Elegy for the Quagga

Krakatau split with a blinding noise
and raised from gutted, steaming rock
a pulverized black sky, over water walls
that swiftly fell on Java and Sumatra.
Fifteen days before, in its cage in Amsterdam,
the last known member of *Equus quagga*,
the southernmost subspecies of zebra, died.
Most of the wild ones, not wild enough,
grazing near the Cape of Good Hope,
had been shot and skinned and roasted by white hunters.

When a spider walked on cooling Krakatau's skin,
no quagga walked anywhere. While seeds
pitched by long winds onto newborn fields
burst open and rooted, perhaps some thistle
flourished on the quagga's discarded innards.
The fractured island greened and hummed again;
handsome zebras tossed their heads
in zoos, on hired safari plains.
Who needs to hear a quagga's voice?
or see the warm hide twitch away a fly,

see the neck turn, curving its cream and chestnut stripes
that run down to plain dark haunches and plain white legs?
A kind of horse. Less picturesque than a dodo. Still,
we mourn what we mourn.
Even if, when it sank to its irreplaceable knees,
when its unique throat closed behind a sigh,
no dust rose to redden a whole year's sunsets,

no one unwittingly busy
two thousand miles away jumped at the sound,
no ashes rained on ships in the merciless sea.

Valhalla Burn Unit on the Moon Callisto

When Jupiter shields Valhalla impact basin
from the light of the small white sun
  and the streaming particles of its wind,
the patients who are able may come
  and linger in the courtyard,
with its soothing views of a thoroughly fireproof world—
concentric rings and ridges of ice and stone
  to the black horizon.
The patients move with exquisite care,
  never too close to each other or to anything,
sipping bottled oxygen,
dressed, where they can be covered, in white
  cotton shifts and strips of gauze.
Even those with eyebrows and lashes
  appear to have two holes burned in their faces.
The doctors who watch them are not old,
  but their faces are slack and soft as worn denim.
Each qualified for this post by the loss
  of an irreplaceable love;
they aren't homesick for an Earth they could ever go back to.
There's room in them now for oceans of understanding,
and they see the use for severe burn victims
  of these conditions—
feeble light, mild gravity, ice-covered ground,
no touch of air to dread.
No atmosphere. That's why the sky is black
  all day, which does tend to bother the nurses,
  the aides, the kitchen staff, the housekeeping crew,
  all of whom are encouraged to miss their planet,

and when they cry, are to do so hunched
over sterile vials meant to preserve
the healing proteins found in common tears.

Scapegoat of Eske's Field

There came a year the potatoes in Eske's Field
grew twisted in the ground, like men buried alive,
and the sky at night bore a new white scar
low over the north hills, pointing down.
One child was born alive that summer,
and that one had a forked tooth in its mouth.
There was nothing to do but pour mead on the stones,
burn comfrey, and brace for trouble.

People began to remember their dreams;
we told one another of beasts with wings, of plague and flood,
a hundred ways the curse could bend, like a snake.
And we milked our goats, hauled water and peat.
The potatoes were good, the baby grew strong,
our cheeses in their rough coats ripened,
lost things were found, but every day
we looked left and right, eyes wide as if it were dark.

That child was a man grown and cutting peat
when they found a haunch, then the rest of a man
like a leather sack, deep in the bog. His head was broken,
his throat cut deep with a noose around it,
and in his mouth were poison bird's-foot leaves.
His hands were bound, his eyes shut, and his face
wore a look we barely recognized,
of one who knows he has nothing more to fear.

From the Elephants' Graveyard

Seeking its own level,
the circus elephant's memory
seeps from the mound
that was its body, cooling
in a borrowed barn in Georgia.

Days of rain, days of no water.
Rumbling pleasure, misery, slow healing.
Smells. Routines. The beloved others.
One man's face, tipped into her weak eyes
over and over for years.

An unseen rivulet,
thick as tar distilled
from a forest's record of rings,
it slips through the straw
and the tired farmyard clay,

through compacted layers of marl and schist,
crystal ribs of lizards
and limestone caverns nursing echoes,
and it joins the oily stream
from the elephants' graveyard—

the secret of whose map-defying location
is that it's everywhere.
Slower than oblivion,
the river winds past
buckled roots of mountains,

slides between rock plates
seamed with disaster,
works through the restless mantle, and feeds
the burning core
that dumbly keeps us warm.

Starlings on the Line

One hundred European starlings
released in Central Park discovered America,
settled its apple trees and woodpecker nests,
but the fifty or so let loose in California
earlier, in the prosperous 1880s,
failed to thrive. Too small a flock, perhaps,
or too bewildered. What season was it?
Time to hunt snails and spiders, or look for
cherries, or hawthorn and holly?
Too much newness—
scorpions and lemons.
Ultramarines, infracrimsons,
high-pitched shades of gold. The last four
hunched in a row on a telegraph wire
for a couple of days, then opened their wings
and shrank into desert sky,
trailing their new-learned songs:
dot dash dash dot
dot dash dot dot
Please come home
Ma sick
Sailing Tuesday next
Need authorization
Need contract
Need your assurance
Please send two hundred
by mail by rail by August please
explain please inform please remit please return
please please please
dot

dot dash
dot dot dot
dot

Flukes

Lacking the patience and limitless godly eyes
to watch every tick of circumstance, every
budge of a molecule or two
that adds up to light rain, a rockslide,
Dutch elm disease, or a fertilized egg
and bright red hair like her great-grandmother's,
we can be surprised, again,
and call the surprise a "fluke": a word
for an accidentally good stroke with a billiard cue,
or the tail of a whale—especially a white one,
cleaving the sea with a sound to our puny ears
like a cataclysm, world derailed.
A minute's deviation from trusty asphalt,
and a red ant, copper glint in the sun,
is braced on the windy hood of a Buick
bearing it irrevocably from its home.
The Buick's driver, who always takes Market Street,
today for no special reason turns left on Mendenhall,
the very street where a red-haired kid
has no one to play with except a ball
named One-Sixteenth, her favorite number.
In the game of this afternoon,
One-Sixteenth, thrown a certain way, strikes
the slab of sidewalk tilted by roots
of an elm tree blighted and chopped down in the sixties,
so the vectors of girl and ball intersect in the street.
What could it look like to our eyes but a fluke
when the Buick with its puzzled ant
arrives three minutes too late, or six too early,
to coincide with the girl, and just keeps going?
So her mother has a good meal inside them

and rockslide fear saved up instead
for the moment during after-supper TV
when the kid sits up from her sprawl on the couch
in a white-lipped wave of amazement
at the headache beating inside her head—
bouncing, crashing against her cracking head,
making her keen her own siren all the way to Emergency,
where, with no time for niceties,
barely sterile they go straight in for the poison leaf,
renegade vein. Afterward, in wet calm,
successful fingers fit back the ragged scalp
and seam the hair with blue thread.
Her mother in a plastic chair
has shredded a magazine and holds the pieces.
They fall when she hears her name, and springs to attention,
and the bare, divided trunk of a whale
slides down away from the surface, well beyond fathoming.

Beyond Rubies

He knew from his studies that some other cultures
adore for their beauty women cross-eyed and fat,
prize wood above gold, or remember and save
every detail of their dreams upon waking;
a missionary in the field must never assume
he knows what people value. One translator
of Scripture had to call Jesus the Pig of God.

The language of the Tlhorh is tonal,
monosyllabic until quite recently,
every syllable depending on pitch for several meanings.
The challenge to its wits is to avoid puns,
to its poets to sidestep rhymes,
to its composers to find themes or motives
that don't sound like mere eccentric speech.

His first sermon was a catastrophe:
He introduced himself as a glorious fish.
Fortunately, a figure of fun
is hard to dislike, unthreatening—
especially when he spends months in his cot
with a local bug his body has trouble translating
and, eventually, with pencils and piles of pages.

When he rendered Matthew 6:20 in Tlhorh—
"But lay up for yourselves treasures in heaven"—
in under one hundred words, without scatological echoes,
tears sprang to the Queen Mother's eyes, and she gave him
a sackful of perfectly spherical rosy agates
polished by the river. He was a millionaire,
as long as he never went home.

The Museum of Damaged Art: Audio Guide

Welcome to the Museum of Damaged Art,
an ever-growing monument
to the intersection of circumstance with design.
One reminder before you begin the tour:
The exhibits are not interactive.
To quote our chipped plaque from the Weatherspoon Gallery,
"The cleanest hands have a coating of perspiration
which is acidic and will damage works of art.
Fingerprints eat into metal.
Stone, textiles, and wood absorb dirt and oil.
Marble and bronze are susceptible
to staining from human touch. Paint is often brittle..."
We do not encourage additions to the collection.
Nevertheless, even as you proceed
to the ground-floor galleries, moist breath, light,
and the mildly abrasive passage of time
increase the scope of our holdings.

Vandalism, of course, plays a part.
The works in our atrium suggest
that attacks by madmen, who claim the art struck first,
are on the rise, along with sheer carelessness.
Michelangelo's *Pietà*,
Mary's forearm smashed and smooth face chipped.
Rembrandt's *Night Watch*, splashed with acid.
A mountain of stone that used to be
a mountain of stone engraved with two weathering Buddhas.
Painting by Barnett Newman: slashed.
Painting by Kazimir Malevich:
green dollar-sign sprayed on.
And these gold bars are all that's left

of intricate ancient Mesopotamian images,
made from the melted treasure of conquered cities.
A forty-inch scratch on Frederic Church's *Icebergs;*
a ballpoint mark on a Matisse.
A broken air conditioner flooded
Brice Marden color fields, and they bled.
A portrait of Eubie Blake was slit
across the face as its shipping crate was opened.

But modern perversity isn't our only source.
Headless Nike is here, Venus disarmed,
the Sphinx, Angkor Wat sunk in vegetation,
terra-cotta Chinese warriors gnawed
by forty varieties of mold.
Down this hall of Florentine frescoes
gray below the high-water mark
is our new Assisi Basilica feature,
"After the Double Earthquake."
The sky shows through the ceiling and walls.
The floor is covered with mattresses.
Watch as long as you wish, and see
if this is the day the blackened Apocalypse
and beloved Sunset Madonna fall to pieces.

Leonardo has a gallery to himself.
Stop this tape for a moment to hear
the whisper of pigment raining from *The Last Supper.*
From left: Ginevra's sawed-off portrait,
the melted man-beast faces of *Anghiari,*
the knots and branches of the Sala delle Asse—
painted over, uncovered, repainted, stripped.

This pile of clay was a monumental horse
meant to be copied in bronze, but riddled
instead by playful French archers.

We have an Egypt's worth of fractured figures,
beautiful lips under crater noses,
an empire of Greek and Roman torsos,
warehoused fingers and phalli.
Our aquarium brims with sunken shipments.
Under glass in the Indian manuscript room
lie individual heaps of powdered pages,
the work of scribes and white ants. Number 412
illustrates the redistributive pattern
of a curator's sneeze.

In this room, test your aesthetic sense.
The twenty-foot-tall giraffe,
cut onto a sandstone outcrop and polished
eight thousand years ago, bears the scars
of projectiles. Visitors tend to honor
ancient target practice and scorn the Victorian.
Can you tell which is which?

Through this bulletproof window
you can glimpse our counterrestoration labs,
where the conservation of damage goes on.
Here, for example, we removed from the *Pietà*
Mary's prosthetic arm. Her wound is our history.
True, some repair may be classified
as damage itself, in which case we try to preserve it.
The work is no more exacting than the decisions.

If we had funding, we could show
Rembrandt's *Danaë* in a time-lapse sequence:
first overcast with age, then bubbling and running
with sulfuric acid, then propped while a row
of curators gently spit water on it,
finally with its monotone repainting.
As it is, just another vandalized Rembrandt, Gallery Five.

Step through the door marked EXIT now;
the cracked sidewalk leads to Parking.
Observe on your left the beaten grass
where not one stone is left on stone
of the building that stood here once, before ours,
and on your right the city skyline
and distant mountains, faint in the corrosive haze.

The Invention of Comfort

From the first, in seas and on mucky land,
creatures moved too fast and died too quickly
to notice, but all around them, in them,
novelties sloshed and budded. Eyes, lungs, sleep, fear.
Structural reinforcement
of the vertebrae in a tail, serrated edges
of a carnivore's teeth, a velvet of capillaries spread
over panels jutting from a slow-moving hummock.

Here pillars of flesh pursue mountains of flesh,
scaly necks heave faces with lidless eyes
to the glare overhead, and, dodging underfoot,
something small has grown armor on its thorax,
or a long and flexible sting,
something smaller has worked out camouflage,
something tiny secretes a burning poison,
and something else has a wet and wiggly nose,

but chiefly it has hair. It has been learning
about tangles and mats and waking with squashed
and rubbed-up fur on the side it likes to sleep on, and that with regard
to working the hind spurs as combs there is
one right way and several wrong. This is the ancestor
of a girl in knee-sprung yellow pajamas
hugging her flattened bear. We know because
when at night the creature curls up

to the lullaby of the springy sound in its guts,
it fits its tail around the tender nose
to hoard warmth, but also to smell itself,
and it rubs its downy bellyskin against its feet

in an unnecessary movement to be known as nestling:
a refinement of the urge to avoid sheer misery
that is worthy of admiration,
which will not be developed for ages.

Why We Held On

In the twenty-third century maybe they'll find
that a parasite made me behave this way—
that just as viruses, flukes, and worms
are implicated in human obesity, heart attacks,
forms of dementia, and possibly
a taste for hot peppers, or keeping too many cats,
a microorganism infests a number of us
and compels us to cling to the past.

Its victims, we imagined we followed our hearts
as we dug up nubbins of brick, aired moldy buffalo robes,
sailed away to stuff birds or copied the letter
that mentioned Granny's mules were named Huldy and Tom.
Saved, preserved, displayed
the leavings of people we couldn't get back,
wouldn't see again or never saw—
the photo that happens to show his chin,
the beaten-copper mask in her grave,
the painting of what they hunted,
the footprint beneath.
Collected the animal parts that last,
that weren't soft or small or delicate, that were
heaped in spate at the bends of rubbed-out rivers.
And mapped the rivers, traced the watershed,
named the ancient sea.

It did us no good, except for illusory
satisfaction, increased our labors,
distracted us from making new things and cleaning,
fostered oppressive accumulations
and melancholy. But it wasn't our fault.

We know that when the three-spine stickleback fish
has a particular tapeworm in its guts, and the worm
to proceed with its cycle must move to a bird,
the worm can turn the fish orange, and make it
swim fearlessly at the surface, almost
begging a heron to eat it. Likewise
a tiny crustacean, unwitting host
to young thorny-headed worms, craves light
when it should seek darkness, and shows itself
to the duck that will eat it,
in which the worms will mature.

The ant whose system is ruled by lancet flukes
never questions the reckless urge
to climb to the tip of a tall blade of grass and stay
as long as the cool of the evening—or
until it is munched by a cow, in whose body
the flukes will thrive. And the housefly filled by a fungus
knows only that it must land in a high place,
and dies there obligingly in an odd position
suitable for the firing of spores at sunset.
But the reasoning minds of the twenty-third-century institute,
having found the cause of our counterproductive affliction,
can move ahead toward a cure. Although
some researchers instead will find
they cannot resist pursuit of the abstruse mystery
of the parasites' motivation.

PART II

The Kingdom of Nab

The Ruins of Nab

Scurry and hunch, snick of incisors
gnawing on stone and anything softer,
scrabbling sift in the seed-hoard,
needle squeak of hairless purple pups.
So for ages jerboas extended their maze
through the ruin that was the city of Nab,
shredding papyri, sanding down their teeth
on broken oil lamps, working stoppers from jars,
and burrowing through the foundations,
which is how the tablet bearing the prayer
of Ashur-tutu-trezzar-esh v
toppled down a crumbling tunnel
and landed on its shattered edge
in the level of Gurna-bodriar III,
confounding archaeologists for years.

During the reign of Ashur-tutu-trezzar-esh v,
nothing much happened, as far as we can tell.
No wars with Egypt or Assyria,
no monuments to extravagance,
no plague. The king was fond of small brown olives
and the fragrance of cassia. He loved his wife.
Sandstone statues of the royal couple
flanked the courtyard. His hive of gold, with golden bees
and honeycombs, was famous among the neighbors.
His subjects went on adjusting to the idea
of writing, adding, subtracting,
and paying taxes. They worshiped in a mud-brick temple
with linen hangings; they lived in mud-brick houses
and kept their records on clay, as if they didn't care
that their lives might not outlast them.

The conversion of Nab from city to ruin,
ascribed to innocent Time, is of course the work of trade routes,
drought, scouring winds, jerboas, and salt.
Salt leaches out of bricks and blooms on their faces;
the sapped walls may collapse at a touch
or the cries of high-circling birds. The statues
of the king and his wife moaned at sunrise,
finally lay down in an earthquake, and gave away pebbles.

The glorious hive was stolen and melted down,
except for three gold bees that fell in a corner
and made their way underground with burrowing wasps,
beetles that lined their manifold halls
with mica-flakes of chiton, and the snake
whose perishing skeleton, found beneath the granary,
was coiled around all three.
Thus says the prayer of Ashur-tutu-trezzar-esh v
to the Storm God: "Your might, Most Powerful One
[or "Destroyer"], makes me small
[literally, "makes me as a jerboa"], yet,
although a grain of sand [or "a thousandfold"], I give thanks—"
For what, we don't know. The rest is powder.
It could be a merely conventional prayer,
one surviving of hundreds. At least we no longer
attribute it to his warrior ancestor Gurna-bodriar,
son of Ashur i, or perhaps his uncle.
We prod and whisk and deduce what we can
from marks in clay, from the trace of a wall.
But the way the king tossed and caught his adoring daughters,
the foolish songs he improvised for his wife, and his furry voice—
these have been safely forgotten.

The So-called Singer of Nab

They have left behind the established cave
with its well-worn floor. Scholarship impels them
in hundreds, but generally one by one,
to find an unknown passage or scrape out their own.
Proto-Semitic linguistic theory,
Hittite stratigraphic anomalies,
microclimatic economics. "What do you see?"
invisible followers ask in their ears,
and they whisper "Wonderful things" as they quarry
a grain of rock at a time, or examine
a fleck of ore, or measure
the acidity of a trickle of water.
See! Behold! Look! Lo!
they cry in season, rapt, in love,
chipping away with their pocketknives,
pencils, rulers, fingernails,
but some have tunneled so narrowly and deep
that those behind see nothing but slivers of light
around an excavator's haunches.

A battered piece of a tablet is all that remains
of the so-called Singer of Nab.
Circa 1200 B.C.E.,
he impressed, or had impressed, some words in clay.
He may have composed a religious hymn,
praise to the king, a poem of love,
an inventory of cattle. (*He* may have been *she*,
but this is unlikely.) The lines we have
could be the beginning or the middle;
there may have been ten more, or hundreds.
The word before this gap, in fact, means "hundreds."

Hundreds led in battle, hundreds slain?
A thousand times beloved, nine hundred sheep?
And the standard translation of this word, here,
is either "desire" or "need." But did he write
of a boundless yearning, or mercantile requirements?
Was he a "singer"? The scholars who care disagree.

Look at them, crouched in a long tunnel dug
by means of argument over an antique syntax,
warming their hands at a chunk of brick
baked maybe in the time of the Trojan War,
broken some moment between then and now—
peering at it with penlights, squandering eyesight.
They know they may crawl out hungry, mumbling,
aged and gray, clutching a secret message of small import
or nothing, nothing. They seem lost. They seem happy.

Unreliable Narration

Of Mina-sarpilili-anda ii,
the only surviving record
is this splendid bas-relief in which
he presses the neck of his Hittite foe
beneath one battle-shod foot
while minions shoulder the spoils
of a conquered city.

          In fact
there was no war that year; a bored stone-carver
was looking for preferment. He received
an allowance of good wine.
In a perfumed cloud of dust
that loitered over the plain,
Hittite ambassadors came to the king
with golden bells and rosewater candy,
birds in cages and spotted cats,
and departed in peace. The king was beloved,
laughed often, feared nothing, and died in his bed
of poison.

          A carnelian image
of his second-best wife,
accurate to the last mole, was plucked
from the dirt by a boy tending goats, sold,
and spirited out of the country, rolled in a rug,
on a ship that sank on a cloudless day.
An image of his first wife, in chrysoprase,
lies tightly packed in buried rubble
for the next generation of archaeologists—

should they prove worthy,
persistent,
and slyer than goatherds.

Certainties

Then I fell upon the city of Makris with my army behind me,
and I made its men cry out in fear at the sight of my splendor
in the aspect of Hasht, in the triple aspect of Nummis. Their
arrows I spurned and their spears I struck aside, and the soldiers
of Erem-eser king of Makris became as rubble before me. Then
I made Erem-eser and all who heard his voice submit to my feet,
and I imposed upon them tribute...

So Nadine reads for the hundredth time,
slouched at her tippy table—the piece of cardboard
meant to be under the short leg is gone again.
The text is called the Boast of Gurna-bodriar III,
the Warrior King, circa 1300 B.C.E.,
who made modest Nab a respectable kingdom.
He vanquished neighboring Makris. He ground
the city of Mishgath-Tera between his palms.
He received fine gifts of placatory friendship
from Adad-nirari I of Assyria,
Kadashman-Turgu the Kassite king,
and the grand vizier of Elam: gold and silver,
of course, dyed wool, elephant hides and concubines,
camels, chairs inlaid with ivory, et cetera,
et cetera, except—
here's this wretched, obscure but not unavailable
translation from the Megiddo ivories
(done before she was born, and stored
in a few libraries all this time),
suggesting that the so-called Warrior King,
at the time of his supposed conquests, was eight years old,
the regency held by his mother. Poor Makris
may have been bludgeoned only by diplomats.

Nadine hears her thesis crumbling instead.
The evidence from Megiddo might be misleading;
the evidence from the sites so far
could support either version. But if we're not sure,
not even sure we can ever be sure,
just like her physicist brother, flopping
through trapdoors into philosophy,
why inch along nearsighted on our knees
from question to question?

The minutes that follow weigh on her like stones.
So that's one reason: to make these stones move on greased rollers
into a pile, sometimes even
a lasting one with a point. At least
to get them off your chest. Somehow,
between one and the next, still facing
her stupid, historically insignificant,
cheap, much-used wooden table,
she releases a long-held image of herself
raising up some broken thing, saying,
"O undone fragments, I shall make you whole."

But what about this regent queen?
If someone else was winning battles for Nab,
how inconvenient for her to give him the credit.
Nadine peels apart her jaw and cupped hand.
Papers stir with her long exhalation.
O messy fragments, here am I.
And here is Gurna-bodriar,
what's left of him, boy or braggart or both.
She leans on the table, feels its familiar lurch.

It may be an artifact of atomic particles
that are themselves almost entirely empty space,
bombarded by the conditions of quantum physics,
but so far she feels sure her elbows can count on it,
even when she's not looking,
to act like a table. A gimpy table.
She picks up a pencil of emptiness in fingers full of space,
and begins to leave on the Boast a new graphite trail.

More Than Water

She was only putting things in her song
to make it longer—
"Dolly-doll,
I love you more than playing battle,
I love you more than apricots,
I love you more than my yellow dress,
I love you more than fish,
I love you more than water—"
but her mother slapped her mouth, twice.
She didn't know why, then,
or why they served so little for supper
and stared at the dish
as though it might be angry.
She hadn't been in the fields to see
the line of mud, like a dead snake,
shrinking in the water-ditches.

Makris Is Fallen

The dog came back,
grinning and smelling of carrion,
and her husband behind it, stride and gestures
too large for the house. His field voice, cracking,
declared a wider kingdom,
and the name of a fallen city,
not theirs this time.
From outside the roar and shrill
of celebration poured in.
He drew near in a rank cloud, breathing hard,
to show her the gash in his thumb.
So she washed in five waters and went to their bed,
but he slept without moving,
still in his cloak and dust.

Irrigation

Are they angry because they are thirsty?
In a dry land pounded down at too many crossroads,
do babies grow up lacking minerals for contentment?
Despite bifocals, Nadine's eyes stop seeing
the inky news unfurled in her hands.
The desert, how many inches
has it encroached this morning, while she
translated dents in clay tablets
from that country's silted layers?
Records of satisfactory harvest, tallied
by the predecessors of the furious ones.
She pictures clever, up-to-the-minute ancients,
patiently drawing water up
their little handmade wheels of stairs
into thousands of ditches laid out for its progress,
to split their tiny hard seeds, to raise their pale naked seedlings—
pictures water pulled backward into their fine fertile arid soil,
and buried salt rising behind it.

Sparrow

No pyramids here, no faces of shadowed gold.
Just a mound of dirt by a pit.
No trucks and tour buses
rattling statues in undiscovered tombs.
One measly adjunct professor, swinging his heels
in a trench he lacks permission to extend.
A sparrow—do they have plain sparrows here?—
hops toward him on its spring-bent legs,
desiring the end of his mashed bean sandwich.
How neatly each of its detailed feathers
lies where it belongs on the twitchy body.
He searches his pockets for cigarettes.
Forty-eight hours to leave the country,
where politics with old, knotted roots
have broken out—like fire, like disease—
to interfere with his dig.
While he's gone, efforts at cultivation
will sap what's left of the water table.
And looters—nothing long interrupts the looters.
He watches the bird lunge forward and strike
his tossed bread offering, twice, three times,
and takes out his talismanic memory:
discovery in the backyard of a bird's skeleton
about the size of his nine-year-old hand,
articulated, whole, white on the dirt.
The minute fitted curves of ribs and wings,
finished claws, skull tapered to beak,
the radiant, concentrated utility,
branded his brain's back wall.
It made him want to know everything.
"Everything" wasn't listed, however, in university catalogues.

He learned to draw from isotopes in ancient human bones
clues to what the people had been eating,
or how to tell from teeth of gazelles
during what season they'd been killed,
or how to interrogate phytoliths—
tiny fossil scraps from plants—
for information on old soil and water.
He kicks against the side of his
deceptively empty ditch. No cigarettes left.
He drags in air, but can't decide
whether to release a laugh or a sigh.
Where the skeletons of dwellers in ancient houses,
intimate with the hearth, lie undisturbed,
gravity has powdered their ribs
with soot they couldn't cough out,
that stayed for centuries after their lungs dissolved.
He scrapes a hollow illegally with one finger.
Someone said someone said fires are burning
in the north and along the highway.
He has thirty-six and a half hours left.
The sparrow regards him with a saurian eye.

The Graves of Mishgath-Tera

Weeds gave the graves away. Where the dead
of Middle and Late Kingdom Mishgath-Tera were buried,
the usual straggling gray-green blades
surrounded oblong patches of deeper green
with deeper roots where once the earth
had been gouged out, jumbled, and pushed back in.

Used through the reign of Ulisek, we think.
Not much to go on—no wig-helmet
of beaten gold, showing hair in a topknot
and fine whorl-tucks of ears; no myths
in cartoon panels, lapis and mother-of-pearl;
not even cylinder seals.

In a covered bowl, a residue of lentils.
In a sealed jar, the stain of sesame wine.
Green blobs mark where objects of bronze were laid;
things made of silver left a purple dust.
Clay cores, almost featureless,
were images of tutelary gods.

Teeth but no bones remain of bodies
whose children vowed to remember them forever.
Crumbs of offering-vessels litter the surface.
This is what we are granted,
something, never enough, as always,
our questions answered with questions.

⌗ ⌗ ⌗

The scribe of Mishgath-Tera whose twelve teeth
are now in a plastic bag labeled 15-04
carried his share of grief and ritual jugs.
He knew that "forever" as a unit of measure
impresses only the living.
He recorded names:

For every descendant of the first clay mixed
with dragon blood, he wrote a name
on a plain clay tablet at the birth,
and sometimes a new name later. Marriage
and other transactions required more tablets.
And when a body was wrapped in its mat

and the grave-diggers made their deep mark in the dirt,
the scribe took his seat, bending his neck
as the name in its inhabitant-form
was dictated for the last time. He wrote,
tipping the stylus in his fingers,
barely moving his lips, and that writing

was sealed in folded clay, which was
imprinted in its turn and permanently
added to the majestic accumulation
of the city archive, represented today
by this right angle, shaded by weeds,
these two nubbins of wall.

Return of the King

Ashur-tutu-trezzar-esh III,
by favor of every god the monarch of all he surveyed,
ruled well for thirty years and died swiftly
in victorious battle. He knew the joys
of fourteen wives in chambers of cedar and linen,
the reward of obedient sons. Never once
did rakes reach the dust of his granary floors.
Never once did he lack roast meat or honey,
figs or good wine, or the pleasure of song,
or the pleasure of making a new song,
if he chose. The remains of his body were laid in richness.

After three thousand two hundred twenty-odd years
at the endless banquet in splendor
where dwells the sun, King Ashur
summoned one of his painted clay servants.
"I looked down," he said, "and beheld the face
of a living man shining brighter than these.
Go find me the cause." And his servant returned
from his errand in puzzlement, saying, "My Lord,
he was eating a ripe tomato."

                    Therefore
was the first reincarnation of a ruler of Nab
born on a truck farm in North Carolina,
imperious red face scowling,
mouth wide open.

The Kingdom of Nab

Dig at Iskot

On the last full day before we had to start loading
for Istanbul and Pittsburgh,
another game-set came to light,
this one in "the corner house."
We know they played with carved figures or painted pebbles
on a wooden game board, probably one against one,
with no apparent sacred or vatic connection,
but was it Candy Land for the kids,
or a game to keep old men parked on benches,
or a tournament of furrowed brows
and long pauses for an emerging batch
of intellectuals who could afford the time?

Now to spend a winter of short days
chewing on what we found and didn't find.
Iskot, a prosperous Nabbite town,
houses, granary, irrigated fields,
temples to Nummis, Eppi, and A'a,
according to these orts. But what was it like?
Never mind Bible-movie scenes
of sheep in the streets and people in tunics declaiming;
how was it? And why didn't someone ask
before the river shifted its course,
before the earthquake, before half the center
was grubbed up and carted away?

Before the temples were looted, the stelae smashed
and used for fill. Only after my father died
did I hear the story of how he was playing catch
one afternoon, nine years old, with the maid—
she'd pitch it out the back door and go on working—

but she looked out and saw the ball in the grass
because without a word he'd gone running
up the mile road to the preacher's house,
and he joined the church that Sunday. What
went through his head? We get to stare at
a clutch of pebbles, a board reduced to a layer of film
a sigh could obliterate. All of us are orphans.

Reconstruction of Temple Area, Seventh Level

The tooth in her hand from the left side of her mouth
reminds Nummis-tet she is aging,
and she sighs into the swatch of wind on her face.
More than three hundred times her servant-name stands
in the records beside the amount of wool doled out
from the stores of the god, and the length, pattern,
and quality of the cloth she made for him,
and her month's allowance of spelt and barley,
dates, cheese, and cooking-butter.

Her hands are supple with wool-grease, callused
from spinning and weaving. Sometimes still
it is joyful service, but "grudging fingers
clothe Nummis nonetheless," and if the women
gossip or sing bawdy songs when no one else hears,
the weave is just as fine. Near the end
of a dutiful month, with the quota well exceeded,
the painted boards and pebbles might come out
for a few rounds of dogs-and-goats.

Upon an avenue wide as a river
the temple doors open: the tall pair arched
and adorned with copper and gold for entry
with offerings of praise and glorification,
the plain one for those begging favor.
Lapis and jasper encrust the walls of the great room, where,
beyond the drain for poured wine, the image
of great Nummis stands, hawk on his head,
fish in one hand, horned ibex at either side.

But behind his back the temple precinct
is factories and expanding archives,
storehouses swallowing porters with sacks and jars,
a tangle of alleys where even the wind
gets lost and doubles back. Here Nummis-tet
stops, slap against a memory,
and lets out a laughing breath. She was a girl
just high as a ewe's back, her tongue taste-feeling
the raw sore gum where a tooth had been—

the old moment falls open, smell of irrigated earth,
the gray cloth around her neck, heel of bread in her hand,
yellow evening under clouds like hills turned over.
But nothing comes to her, nothing at all,
of what she did or knew before or after. Why should that be?
Strange as a single brick where a wall once stood,
or just one tablet in place of a full year's records.
How could that be? She watches a wisp of dust,
badgered by wind, rise and walk down the alley.

What They Found

Her grave, but no bones.
Her city, but no houses.
Specks of color, no sound.
Fragments of records, chiefly
commerce and law.

Before they went into the weaving room
with the other girls for the day, Nummis-ri
showed Nummis-tet what was in her hand:
an eggshell, thin freckled ivory,
broken only at one end,
the size of an olive. The dove that laid it
must have bled on the altar already.
They peered inside at the residue
of the birdling's food, or body.

In the room full of wool-motes catching light
and dropping it, they recited with the rest,
"Rejoice in the bounty of Nummis the Mighty!
He has sent us water for our fields,
he has given us good things in plenty.
He has made Iskot the terror of its enemies;
their pride he has humbled, their abundance he has laid waste.
Oh, that we might see—from a safe distance—
his power made manifest!"

Every day the same prayer before work—
Nummis-gir's joke about distance somehow stays in—
no matter how meager the barley, how old the butter.
In a row with Nummis-ri and -gir and -eskar,
feeding the god's thread into his looms,

Nummis-tet almost drops her shuttle
when the cat advances with a mouthful jerking,
its trophy a raider of temple stores,
a rat better fed than anyone in the room.

The cat stills its offering and lays it down;
red drops sink into the floor.
Nummis-tet looks away. That eggshell, suppose you made
its perfect shape in clay the size of an urn
for a stillborn baby? With so many god-servants here,
demand for plain, tiny urns is high:
infants of husbandless mothers are always born dead.
Nummis-ri sends her a watery smile.
Work faster. What would it be like to be a bird?

Her grave, but no eggshell.
Her city, but no cats.
Specks of color, no cloth.
We don't know what she looked like.
Neither did she.

Fragments from Rubble

By day he stares at the ground, distinguishing
fragments from rubble, but when at night
he cracks his back he can see overhead as many stars
as the people who lived here and called it Iskot
and thought of their mud-brick cluster as a great city.
The nearest city now, across miles of desert,
lies coiled around its dragon's hoard
of weapons and hospitals, cigarettes, CDs, and water;
otherwise, he thinks, no one would ever go there,
live where the air is scored with sirens,
walk where the sky's intermittent rumble
may or may not be the sound of commerce.
Here his sleep is a tent of thick black felt,
entered only by dreams.
Here he analyzes detritus
that matters, if it matters, only
because it is old, and once intentional.
People under a different polestar,
under a younger sun, who worshiped
a god with a bird on his head and a fish in his fist—
they meant this paving-stone, this flake of enamel.
After a day with his brush in the dust,
when he closes his eyes he still sees unsorted litter.
But once—he'll never tell anyone this—
on his way to sleep, in a weightless dusk
he stood in the trench whose floor was partly
an alley behind the Nummis temple,
and a thin woman wrapped in woven wool,
head high as his shirt pocket, stretched out an arm
and left in his palm
the little bones of her hand.

The Kingdom of Nab

LATE KINGDOM

MIDDLE KINGDOM

LATE MIDDLE

• **EARLY MIDDLE**

EARLY KINGDOM

Destruction

Allsop is fond of quoting Sir Leonard Woolley's
"Excavation is destruction," but he admits
to fantasies of strangling the so-called baron
who spent too much of the nineteenth century
converting portions of Mesopotamia
from sites pertaining to Sumer, Nab, and Assyria
into evidence of his whirlwind passage.

They say the Baron von Hausknecht traveled
nowhere without a valet, a chef, and a mistress,
and cursed in nine languages, some of them dead,
which he taught his mynah bird. He was stout
and well over six feet tall; his pockets
chuckled with rare old coins. Madly rich
and wildly in debt by turns, he left a trail
of women smitten or well amused,
partridge bones and empty bottles,
rumors of duels, a few of his teeth,
and a newly chic fascination with ancient lands.
He wore black lambskin gloves, they say, at all times,
and had crates of fine wine carried to every dig.

His hands were restless. They wanted filling
not to amass or study, but
to spill, to jingle, to give away grandly,
and if they had nothing else to do
his thumbs would rub at the base
of his middle fingers. Carmelita,
a former opera-chorus girl who
dabbled in palmistry, pointed out
he was rubbing mostly the mounts of Apollo and Saturn,

a clear indication he should have been
an artist: melancholy, solitary,
in love with beauty in all its forms—
to which he made the correct reply.
No one knew of the malformed Galateas
he'd carved and smashed to powder; let them instead
admire the bug-eyed, bearded images,
long lost beside the ancient Tigris,
revealed by his new pursuit.
He loomed at the edge of a fresh pit, seized a shovel,
leapt in, and with a single thrust
beheaded a limestone statue of Sililit.

Allsop, seventy-eight years later,
faithfully sifts the unspectacular graves
of Mishgath-Tera, avoiding the gouge
where von Hausknecht did his worst.
He will leave two quadrants untouched, even as
he resists the temptation of pristine Tell Makaira,
just forty miles away. Something must be set aside
for the ones whose coming is foretold:
twenty-first-century scientists with machines,
who will scrape a bowl that once held goat-meat stew
and work out the proportions of honey and fennel,
or tell from a bone the shade of the buried one's hair,
who will reconstruct statuettes from handfuls of crumbs,
and to whom Sidney Sullivan Allsop, he can't help thinking,
will be one more barbarous digger.

Vulture Feather

On a stone step in the conquered city
she hugs herself and rocks, shifting
the weight of grief that could swallow an empire
back and forth and back and forth.
Taken away, light of my eyes.
May I bear a serpent's egg
if I live. Remember this our shame forever.
Till the next warrior drags her away. Later
the stone is dragged off, too, for the city rebuilt,
and against it winds arrange the dust
of that city and its king and its conqueror.
Even the river makes itself a new bed.
Years pass through the dissolving plaza
on camelback, on cloudback, lordly beings
that know only one direction, one pace.
And perpendicular through a few thin minutes,
one gray feather, cupped like an ear,
has fallen a long way. It drifts down ragged
and docks against a chip of marble
the shape of an eye—lies on its spine and shivers,
tips for an afternoon from side to side.

Estimmag and Sililit

Number 81: Tablet from Ab-insa, inscribed with the tale of Estimmag and Sililit. Dated circa 1900 B.C.E., this is the most nearly complete version known of a story whose origins would be much older. Herron and van Niewaal, working independently, each discovered in 1994 that a fragment in the Istanbul Museum of the Ancient Orient fits at the ends of columns 3 and 4 of the inscription. Because of the damaged condition of the surface and two broken corners, portions of the text are still missing or indecipherable; these are indicated by ellipses, or reconstructions in brackets.

...

To his brothers and his milk-brothers and the men of his house
      Estimmag said,
"No one else has sworn to go to the mountains,
No one else has sworn to find Sililit in her seat among the hills,
      to recall to her our tribute and her favor,
      to speak in her presence until she lifts
         the sickness from our houses,
      so it drinks our lives no more.
But come with me, and I will go first,
I will go before you into that land no one has seen.
My foot will walk on that ground, then your feet will walk,
My eye will look on that [place,] then your [eyes will look,]
My mouth will taste that air, then your mouths [will taste."]
...
... her seat on the mountain ...
Her seat among the hills, the stony hills of the holy one
      and her garment,
Where the first root of the Great River lies on her knees,
Where the second root of the Great River lies on her tongue
      and issues from her mouth.
Now as they ...

The fruit of [the trees] hung over their heads,
        within reach.
So they ate, and spat out the pits on the ground,
And when Estimmag had eaten,
        he made to speak, but his tongue was silent,
        his throat released no sound,
And his men had eaten
        and made to speak, but their tongues were silent,
        their throats released no sound.
Now as Estimmag walked and his men walked behind him,
        the orchard they left at their backs,
        and the forest they left at their backs,
But the *uzmim*-plant grew thickly there.
As Estimmag walked and [his men walked] behind him,
The leaves of the *uzmim*-plant brushed against [their] shoulders,
The leaves of the *uzmim*-plant [brushed against] their hands,
And when Estimmag came out from among the leaves,
        he made to raise his arm, but he could not lift it,
        he made to close his hand, but …
And his men came out …
        …
… and gazed on the shining water,
The river that had crossed only five great stones
        since leaving its place at her feet.
And when Estimmag looked up, his eyes were darkened,
        there was darkness before his face,
And when his men looked up, their eyes were darkened,
        and darkness showed itself to [their faces.]
But Mikrek the servant of Sililit came forward
        and led them to the bright goddess,
        to the very station of the holy one and her garment

where she was, with the river and all its mouths
in her possession.
In the presence of Sililit they stood
with their moveless tongues that would not speak,
their arms that would not clasp her feet,
their eyes that saw nothing where they were,
And they fell down before her.
… [Mikrek] said, "…
To find you in your seat among the hills,
to recall to you their tribute and your favor,
to speak in your presence until you lift
the sickness from [their houses,]
so it drinks their [lives no more."]
As he spoke before holy Sililit
they pressed their faces in the dust.
Sililit of the roots of the [Great River]
looked … and said,
"Estimmag, you have … and your …
…
… when you … my garment …
… like little stones of …
… not in vain,
with a groan, with a …"
…
… and when they had passed the shining water,
their eyes began …
… [and when they had passed] the *uzmim*-plants,
their shoulders regained their strength,
…
… on the pavement before the blue doors of her temple,
"Did you come to Sililit and see the … on her necklace

and the lapis-stones at her waist?
Did you clasp her feet, did you cup your hands on her heels
And speak to win her favor?"
But Estimmag …
"… whom I have seen, whom I honor.
The Great River she has not withheld from us;
She has not gone up from her seat among the hills,
     nor drawn back her garment.
The dust lies still on the ground.
She looks on us with favor. Yet her blessings
     come down upon Ab-insa not according to our desire,
     but according to …"
Therefore the people …
     … gather up and …
     even the widow and the infant …
     … as if the smallest grains …

                                The rest is missing.

Sililit the Ungraspable

If they find anything,
who will take possession of it,
and who will decide what it means?
At least eight nations, five religions,
roughly fifteen dozen tribes
have claimed the pale dirt under her boots
since the ancient Nabbite temple of Sililit
stood where Wendy stands. Or near.

"Sililit the Ungraspable," wrote Allsop,
"whose priests and azure temple doors
hid well her mysteries and their purpose.
Goddess of neither love nor war,
fertility nor destruction, she was
strongly associated with the Great River,
but more we cannot say…"
This team is here for more.

As Wendy, kneeling to her plot, picks up
where she left off yesterday, loose thoughts
chip one another in her head:
cave paintings, tomb walls, medieval frescoes
dampened by the sighs of beholders;
evidence destroyed by discovery;
dreamless rest disturbed; errors
set in textbook stone;

money spent on climate control
for historic artifacts under glass
when it could have fed x number of starving children,
whose bodies are highly perishable;

the science of preserving objects
meant to decay; her freshman roommate's
art experiments, many involving
actual and theoretical beelines,
or anthills and the placement
of stones by the artist, or
the diversion of a stream
to run over her body—but now
Wendy rocks back on her bent toes,
clawing for her notebook while staring
at the trace on clay that may have been blue,
that might disappear, that her hands have uncovered.

Every door in every temple of Sililit
was necessarily blue. A blue door
swung open, pushed
by Sifer-ne-naki the acolyte,
wild-eyed, panting, at the end
of his night of initiation.
The others around the room looked up,
remaining seated.

He raised his palms. He thought
of inhaling flames from torches,
of speaking purely in fire.
"She rose from her stone," he cried,
"and all night the river—" How to say it?
"I beheld the opening of her mouth,"
he tried once more,
"and her garment she laid upon me."

They were standing by then,
to surround him with the instruments,
their faces unchanged.
He knelt more or less where Wendy is kneeling,
and knew what she knows:
I have found my desire.
I have breathed on it.
I have bared it to plundering light.

⊡ ⊡ ⊡

The Kingdom of Nab

Twigs and Knucklebones

In the second twelve days since they took up the floor
to bury her grandfather on his side
with a water cup at his mouth, already
she sometimes forgets to make the sign
at the threshold for A'a's protection.
Once in the room, though, she still avoids certain bricks—
but this time almost tramps on them, stumbling
thanks to her little brother's scattered clay horses.
Chewing her tongue, she reaches the front door
and looks out, exactly as no one's supposed to,
not now, when the air could have devils in it.
There's nothing to look at. A few round-eyed doves.
To the north stands the temple of A'a the Unhewn,
but all she can see to the north is blank walls of houses
across the street, and farther east
are newer houses built by families
that had to leave their old ones.

—She lived in Ab-insa, city of A'a,
in the days of its prosperity,
when even the children wore dyed clothes,
before the armies of Iskot came
and led its governor through the streets
robed in a jackass skin.

In 1880, Baron von Hausknecht
fell upon the site, and his men
dug an exploratory trench
that destroyed a significant area
and missed the primary temple of A'a
by twenty feet. Bored with mud bricks

and broken pots, he then took himself off
for Babylon. He may not have been
a baron at all, but was regal, sonorous,
fond of wearing a wide purple cloak,
eager for treasure.
He traveled with a retinue,
an opera-chorus mistress, and always
the mynah bird he had taught to take bread
daintily from his lips, and to cry,
"Bring me silver! Bring me gold!"
and, "Darling, where are the dancing girls?"

Oh, the stories they told of the baron
when he could no longer tell them himself—
until his well-fleshed memory withered reluctantly
to a few twigs and knucklebones.
The trench, the cloak, the bird.

She scuffs one foot on the threshold, over
and over, a little dry half a dance,
humming a half-tune under her breath,
touching the gift of red beads, many
smooth red beads, hung around her neck.
Soon, when she ends her fourteenth year,
she will be a wife, and go to live
with his family in a new house, newly whitewashed,
with new mats on the floor, and no one
buried beneath it.
At least not yet.
At least if she lives so long.

In 1929, McPartland
(lean, sunburned, conscientious McPartland)
carefully sank a vertical shaft
some distance from von Hausknecht's trench
and spent the first of three seasons there.
He it was who proposed the theory
that Nab the city became the royal capital
of Nab the kingdom with varying borders
that sometimes included Ab-insa.
He bored everyone with his pottery-shard
chronologies, until he discovered
the gold of Gurna-bodriar.
So he left a few knucklebones, too:
his perseverance, his Lindbergh squint,
his exclamation, "Treasure, men, here!
Look at it shine!"
Or something like that.

Just two streets over, southwise mostly,
the servants reported yesterday,
a girl her own age and the mother
have the spilling sickness, the terrible fever
when everything in your body comes out.
They said if the family has to bury
two or three more, their tomb will be full
and their house will have to be left behind.
She knows of two houses like that
not far from here. But not who lived in them,
not who lies in them still.

The team for the 1999 season
came with a ton of equipment and beer.
They flickered a minute on public TV,
a show about modern digging techniques,
but Tom wasn't on the tape. And no,
his former boyfriend was not watching.
"Peanut butter and pickle sandwiches,"
he told a sympathetic ear.
"I kid you not. He loved the things.
And he'd walk around the apartment flossing."
On the morning of taping, Tom was crouched
in a different part of the site, a house
where he'd found two crushed red beads; he was holding
as if it were a baby bird
a small clay horse.

To the west—no one goes that way—
stand almost a quarter of Ab-insa's houses,
their tombs filled, upper floors empty, residents
shifted east, careful not to look back
when they walked out to the prayers. She imagines
that nothing moves there at all, not a snake,
not one lost cat, not even the wind.
That a holy hush without interruption
envelops the walls,
the bodies folded and bricked below
and the infants in jars, forever.
When she leans out, stands on tiptoe, raises her chin,
as far as she can see to her left hand
lies the growing city of the dead.

An Old Joke

Overtaken
by the spilling sickness
thousands of years before the drug
that could have cured her was bottled,
she expelled
clumps, gouts, and puddles of matter
her body had need of
but could not keep.

They buried the husk of her
in the front room,
tiredly crying.

Now that their house and its city
have settled once more to ground level,
will the dust she relinquished
rise on a storm
and blow through Jerusalem or Baghdad?
Or has it sifted down to layers
that don't even shiver
at surface explosions?

She lived sixteen years
before the fever closed on her,
and never spent one second
thinking about this,
or imagining an apprentice scholar
flown from another continent
and thinking about it for her.

On her last ordinary day
she laughed at a joke,
setting in motion
the air you just inhaled.

She licked honey
from her fingers,
and they didn't taste like dust.

Siren

Before the battle raises its voice again,
stragglers hear her keening,
one more rag driven into the ground,
her face a cleft stone
between the shards of her hands.
On the road that will soon be not a road,
nor any longer the way to a city,
she claims her new home:
the red mud that cups her knees.

Jars

So tuck him into a womb of clay.
In the few days he lived outside of mine,
he slept little, cried less, stared at me
as if trying hard to think of the answer
to something I'd asked him.
Last night, he lost interest.
My first son, who required from me
so much to make his little lavender body.
It goes in a jar now and under the floor
in the dark, beside his father's father.
Here is my bracelet to be his necklace.
In one year, my mother, my sister, my son,
and my husband, brought back in pieces from battle,
yet how can I claim to be singled out
by the arrows of Hasht or the mouth of Sililit?
That would dishonor the mourners who sought
the thousand fallen at Nevis-edrasar,
my father who takes up the floor yet again.
On this very street, Mas-artagit-emmen
in the days of his strength turned yellow and died;
after him went Mas-artagris-gal, whose jaw decayed,
and I know of two other infant jars sealed and broken
and placed beneath their mothers' feet.
Break this jar's mouth,
and leave it below to be covered.
Where does it come from, this stubborn idea
that we should decide what we keep?

To the Unhewn

The snake in the dovecote lifts its head
from the egg it is drinking.
The hour of noise has come.
With the smell of wine on stone,
of flat cakes burned to ashes,
of blood poured through a narrow reed,
the unvarying cry: "To the Unhewn,
the Unencompassed, the Ever-Seeing,
Preceding, Co-extant with Darkness,
these gifts. Preserve us." Nothing new,
nothing dangerous. The snake dips again
to its meal. And the watching servant
of A'a the Unhewn makes note of this omen,
whatever it means, and prays.

First

A'a-mnek, by virtue of long service
First Among Those Upon Whose Prostrations
Falls the Gaze of A'a,
sits on a ledge against a wall
and awaits the latest initiate. Hours ago
they left the public part of the temple—
painted walls in swaying lamplight,
scuff and rattle, bay of prayer—
for this quiet passage of brick and stone.
No ornament even upon the door
of the innermost chamber,
where A'a-mit is closeted now with the first
and holiest image of A'a.

He laid his sandals on the floor,
straightened his shoulders, and entered
ready for unimaginable glory.
A'a-mnek watches the sandals curl
slightly around their emptiness,
dark cups impressed by the toes. Few votaries
come to this temple; in wartime
more pledge to Hasht in his lion-drawn chariot,
in peace, to the pleasurable rites
of golden Eppi, and always the courts of Nummis
are raucous with petitioners.
But A'a is oldest, shown to the people
only in the form of a pillar, hung about
with fronds and vines, beasts and birds,
and necklaces of men.

In a chamber scarcely ample enough
for a man to prostrate himself, the novice
stands without an offering
for the first and last time,
forbidden to bow down or avert his eyes.
Before him three channels
lead to three drains in the floor,
one brown with dry dove-blood,
one slick with oil, the third
bare, touched by nothing
but purified water. Beyond them stands A'a,
a rough, slumping finger of stone,
almost the height of a man.
No limbs, no mouth. The eyes
two wide dark pits,
one lower than the other.

A'a-mnek shifts to ease his bad hip.
The time approaches to set out baskets
of pease and bird-meat for the afflicted
who come, almost unobserved, at night.
But first he must greet the initiate,
whenever A'a-mit thinks to turn
and stumble out, like each one before
abashed and silent,
new priest of a god without hands.

Flinders

Flying through almost nothing
toward a planet freshly imprinted
with *Australopithecus* tracks,
a photon takes one path if it is observed
by earthly instruments in 2002 C.E.,
another if it is not. Thus our current techno-futzing
determines the photon's past.
Ruminating upon a world
slung between counterintuitive particles,
physicist John Wheeler postulates
that the cosmos beyond our perceived horizon
is a kind of cloud as yet unresolved,
that the universe exists only, he says,
"with somebody to look at it."

Photons rain unobserved on Gustarz,
crouched at his first dig, sweating into
a crease in the dirt as he patiently makes it deeper.
Perhaps today he will unearth
yet another crushed oil lamp.
Everything they are here for, he thinks,
is fragmented, altered, spoiled, allusive—
except the blank sort-of-stela he found last week.
People lived here, his ancestors maybe,
but the tender parts are gone, the smells,
the sounds, the binding threads. Of course
he began with dreams of gold. Now he'd be
excited by a lousy unbroken pot.

"Still and all," McPartland says if anyone grumbles,
"it's needful, all of it needful."
When, rarely, he isn't busy, he picks up
a pebble and rolls it around in one hand.
He spent last night assembling pieces
the size of his little fingernail
into half a clay vessel. Gustarz
noticed his tent walls glowing at dawn, stepped in,
and saw him regarding the thing with a look
of stern love, as one might a son.

In a city absorbed by the kingdom of Nab,
here stood a temple to an ancient deity
of whom is known no myth, no image,
only that it was called A'a, and oldest.
McPartland theorizes that the cult
dwindled to nothing in a time of plague.
At its height, this wasn't the richest of Nabbite temples,
but its sanctuary was painted in many colors,
lit, it seems, with hundreds of lamps.

Besides the lamps and flecks of paint
they don't have much: a partial floor plan,
and, in the maze of little rooms
behind the large one, the monolith
that Gustarz found, 1.5 meters tall,
which so far has told them nothing.
Its surface isn't even carved,
just naturally eroded, even the deep pits
near the top that, though lopsided,
strike everyone who sees them as two sad eyes. Later,

Jusuf and Keram will find a cache
of arthritic bones, one of several burials:
For the first time in four thousand years,
light will fall on the bundled remains
of A'a-mnek, priest of A'a, the One Who Watches.

Epilogue: Rockpile

post–Late Kingdom

I am Parnisek, spear-hand of Nummis-God-of-Life,
host of his table, slayer of his meat. I am
Parnisek, king, ruler and west wind of Nab, king
of Iskot and axle of all its chariots, king and
foot upon the shoulder blades of Makris, king and
fastening of the shackles that bind Ab-insa,
king who feasts upon the white cakes of Mishgath-Tera,
king and ruler of Elab who seized the stones
of its temples, king and conqueror of Tulifath who turned
the faces of its inhabitants to the ground. The blessings
of Nummis Hawk-Lord pour from my open mouth. The riches
of Nummis Fish-Lord pour from my open hands. The power
of Nummis Ibex-Lord mantles my shoulders. If any man
damage these words, may the eyes in his head
no longer see day and night. If any man shatter these words,
may the bones in his body be shattered. If any man
cause this stela to be crushed, may his head be crushed
and his body be crushed by Nummis-God-of-Life, in whose service
Nab rejoices with all that is in it, so say I, Parnisek the king.

Bits of this inscription, mostly upside down or sideways,
show in the walls of the village where Ati lives,
near the rockpile where they still find, sometimes,
scraps of colored tile for babies to teethe on.
But no one here remembers the city of Parnisek
as anything more than a source of stone,
a place where jerboas multiply, so perhaps
they have evaded the curse unknowing. A broken arm,
a crippled leg, a mashed thumb now and then;
no pattern of disaster. Ati herself
has a husband, two sons, food, and work enough

to drive thoughts out of her head—
making goat cheese, bread, and pottage,
tending the garden, the babies, the clothes.
Her back hurts sometimes. Now. But as she
shoves her knuckles into the ache,
she closes her lips on a foolish smile—
in the dark his fingers found the mole
at the nape of her neck, she touched the scar on his hip.
She has a good husband. Look on the floor
at his fine herd; no matter how many his sons break,
he makes them more little clay horses.
He shouldn't have told them that awful story,
though, to make them behave, the Rockpile Man
they say comes out on moonless nights,
with eyes in his hair, and one of his hands a fish,
reaching, cold—they'll cry tonight. She'll sing to them,
her hands on their knees. Ati walks out,
angles away from the ugly pile,
facing where she can see the most sky come down.
Right now the goodness is rising in her again,
that feeling of holding a fresh warm egg in her hands,
or a warm bowl, or warm husband,
faint sweetness under the tongue as after new bread.
It isn't the pinched-clay gods they plant
with the barley she wants to thank for this,
or the round-bellied stone stitched into her pillow,
or the red sun over the rockpile,
but she wishes to give thanks—though it is
for something she won't keep, that will leave no trace.

PART III

Figs

Look Again

I know how little I know
from observation:
that the dog sleeping on the rug
with pure concentration
will be sleeping, each time I look up,
in a different direction,

that five wart-lidded mushrooms
can form on the lawn
in the time rain takes
to shift from falling to fallen,

that my eyes are too slow
to track shooting stars, too quick
to spy continental drift,
and Earth conceals its spin
by spinning me with it,

that a tree won't let me
see its growth, only its height,
that hairs on my head go singly gray
only by night.

Underground Orchids

Life on this planet persists in knitting its minerals
into animal and vegetable variations, behaving at all times
like the central point of the cosmos,
and because it is water it seeks the paths of least resistance
and pauses sometimes to admire itself,
because it is earth it might subside in camouflage
or darkness or cease to move for its own good reasons,
because it is air it may seem like nothing
yet be the invisible sustenance of oceans or forests or a shade of blue,
and because it is fire it leaps and is uncertain
and leaves smelly waste and goes everywhere it can uninvited.
It presses its lips where boiling sulfur cracks the ocean floor,
swims in acid cavities below the roots of mountains,
burrows and flits and infects and strangles and hatches,
constructs mats, reefs, trunks, tunnels, stained-glass windows,
and ad campaigns for raspberry-scented chinchilla dust.
Mammalian bipeds especially intrude where they are unfit to go,
chewing coca leaves to walk on ridges where oxygen falls away,
training beasts to carry weight in the desert and drinking their blood,
beating seawater back with little hands.
On the southern ice cap, one turns his frozen socks inside out
and shakes his blackened toes into his lap.
In the country he comes from, earth is parched,
air warped with the heat he longs for.
Thirsty flies glue themselves to plants that begin to digest them;
modest orchids bloom underground. In his country
glinting saucers are filling with penicillin
while soldiers don uniforms. There is singing.
A shimmer over cannon mouths. Fire consumes. Mud consumes.
Many stars since they were born
have been sending their light to shine upon us,
but some are rushing away as fast as they can.

From the Files of a Recording Angel

On its birthday there were six billion of it,
pre-animal, pre-vegetable bacteria,
a patch on a young planet,
steadily harvesting water.
Good water, good water, good, good enough,
then too bad. The old story, written here
as a kind of stripe, a kind of bump in stone.

Once, uncounted bushels of jellyfish
(once, and more than once) washed up
on sand above a receding ocean—
armless, heartless, transparent lenses,
giving up to the sun with their substance
half a mile of extravagant shining
that no one saw but seagulls,
half an hour of bright litter before
they dried into wrinkled membrane.
Four left fossil shadows.

Upon the wind-scoured plain, behold,
as proof that grass was here before,
grass, which will provide, as future
evidence of its existence, grass.

Dear Sir or Madam: Enclosed please find
a persistent tactile memory—
the squashy heft of smoked meat wrapped in foil
to take on the plane from my father
(lethal cells in him maybe already building)
to my sweet carnivorous husband.
Best I ever ate, he said.
From the implicated, carcinogenic grill.

I have about six billion fragments like that;
should I throw them in the river? It's full
of salmon shoving upstream to breed and die,
not one of them saying
remember, remember me.

Tell the Bees

Tell the bees. They require news of the house;
they must know, lest they sicken
from the gap between their ignorance and our grief.
Speak in a whisper. Tie a black swatch
to a stick and attach the stick to their hive.
From the fortress of casseroles and desserts
built in the kitchen these past few weeks
as though hunger were the enemy, remove
a slice of cake and lay it where they can
slowly draw it in, making a mournful sound.

And tell the fly that has knocked on the window all day.
Tell the redbird that rammed the glass from outside
and stands too dazed to go. Tell the grass,
though it's already guessed, and the ground clenched in furrows;
tell the water you spill on the ground,
then all the water will know.
And the last shrunken pearl of snow in its hiding place.

Tell the blighted elms, and the young oaks we plant instead.
The water bug, while it scribbles
a hundred lines that dissolve behind it.
The lichen, while it etches deeper
its single rune. The boulders, letting their fissures widen,
the pebbles, which have no more to lose,
the hills—they will be slightly smaller, as always,

when the bees fly out tomorrow to look for sweetness
and find their way
because nothing else has changed.

Briar Rose

On her sixtieth birthday
they pricked her with a syringe,
and granted the dry crust of mercy she fell
into a few days' imitation of sleep.

Containers of soup arrived in the kitchen,
and soft potted plants,
but the leafless vine
with its clutch of roots in her belly

thorn by thorn infiltrated her room,
tapped on the window,
scratched at the ceiling,
tightened crooked arms around her.

Sometimes her eyes stirred
under their covers
as if she sensed
that she should have been dreaming,
until the bramble held to her lips
the single flower that sealed them.

Real Live Boy

And so Pinocchio the wooden puppet
became living flesh,
as he wished. The first

of many surprises. His palms were soft,
sometimes grew wet,
and when a splinter of wood
slid into his skin,

it didn't feel friendly there. Not one
of his eager dreams had mentioned
that a real boy couldn't remove his foot

whenever it broke
and peg on a new one,
or that he wouldn't understand
the fiddle's words anymore.

He was no longer remarkable,
though often amazed
at how the parts of his new spine found

so many ways of aching, or how,
in the pit of winter,
the bellows in his chest grew heavy with phlegm,

how the dog in his belly yelped for bread
when there was none,

how sleep ruled him
when he had meant
to work all night again
on his wooden Geppetto.

Land's End

Like a good Viking
I followed my feet to reach the shore
where the water gives back
no face, no light,
there to board the ship made of my losses:
its hull my nail-parings,
its cables my hair,
its sail my strength, its anchor—
no, not even now
will I say the drowned man's name.

But the water
licked my hands, and the breeze
that cuffed me brought only
a ragged bandanna
and a line of pelicans two feet up,
admiring themselves as they flew.
No fate-ship. No need
for anything I remember.
And a tide forever
leaving things behind.

Day on a Dry Planet

Now, a year before misery, they are
so terribly in love they can last
a day on this airless, waterless,
windless planet, a place so still
the gray ridges of their parallel footprints
will last two million years. At first,
lacking permission as ever
from the others back home,
they hardly know how
to do anything for each other but wait,
wait and look. The tiny sun is high
when they stop discussing the landscape and
she lays a palm on his shirt pocket.
So far away, that sun, or feeble,
a few stars will shine
in the violet sky at noon,
and he and she look as though they've met
in the midnight light of a parking lot again,
eyes black, the space in their mouths
more black, lips sallow,
green sparks curled in their hair. But
no haze here—she can see
the cotton stripes under her fingers beating
more clearly than anything, ever,
and when he presses her other hand,
not a molecule comes between them.
Fatally, they learn to believe
in such closeness. Meanwhile
moisture is leaving their skin,
but they don't need it yet.
Spread beside them is picnic chicken,

even a foolish cake, but they can't
let go to eat; they kneel facing each other
this way so long that
first he is on her dark side,
but later, pale, she is on his.
Then they rise, one-tenth
of their earthly weight,
the dust they disturb
falling lightly where it will stay
for eons. They waltz.
A box-step at first,
these two who have never danced,
treading the same prints over and over,
but no one, at last, is watching;
together they sway into curves and swirls,
no music in this vacuum
but desperation, and their feet
mark a daisy chain down the valley.
Closer and closer they spin, defying
centrifugal force;
laughing though sound is impossible; closer
and slower; they slowly stop laughing;
they almost stop time.
But when they run back
to their freeze-dried chicken,
wine fading from their glasses into the sky, they catch
a glimpse of the three-second sunset,
the sharpening dark.

After they are dragged back, appalled,
to oxygen, gravity, and mist,

a salt-crusted tissue will shrivel beside
the crater where a splash of wine fell
near the indentations of four knees.
They will last in this desert place
almost as long as hopeless error,
almost as long as loss.

Loving a Saint

When orphaned baby raccoons swarmed into his sleeves
she knew she loved him;
when they stole her earrings and washed the checkbook
and left buttered pawprints all over the house
she marveled at his patience.
Knowing his place would be crowded,
since his benign door would shut nothing out,
she followed him home—
how not to crave the light of his eyes,
the presence of one who honored all creatures?
Who made no distinction between her yappy dachshund
and his pound dog stinking with cancer,
or a mangy murderous quivering stray,
or the fleas on his arms, or the fleas on her legs,
or the slugs that brightened the doorstep every morning?
She already knew that neighborhood cats
abandoned the hunt to follow him,
but hadn't foreseen the jumping spiders,
the woodpeckers knocking on the window frames,
the millipedes in bed, the worms in his pockets.

Later she came to see that the shine in his gaze
when it rested on her
was the same as when he looked at day-old chicks
or a nervous skunk.
She had thought she was good at sharing.
She found herself niggling away at questions
like why he addressed a rotifer as "brother"
but looked down her swollen throat and said "Sister Strep."
She developed a fondness for rocks, and felt
nostalgia for slapping mosquitoes. Then

he'd fondly pat his belly, and hers, after breakfast
and thank their digestive bacteria,
and she'd melt.

Tonight while he's outside
giving their lentil loaf to some deer,
she gropes in the pouch of her kangaroo heart
for perfect love that casteth out resentment,
hunger of various kinds, and fear
of the three-legged alligator, tired apparently
of dragging its belly around the house
but watching her from the corner,
fear of the long dry rustle she heard in the wall before dawn
when the mice were asleep.
She wakes in the night, or dreams she does,
sees two eyes with a moon-cool gleam,
and more than anything wants to know whose they are.

Streamlined

Though books have been sent to the ocean in generous numbers,
no squid to our knowledge has ever consulted a book;
though scattered showers of cash and heirlooms
fall through that domain, no squid has ever
worn its grandmother's diamond ring
or left restrictions on the family fortune.
Squid children know what they need to know
though they've never met their elders;
squid children have what they need
although their relatives give them nothing, accumulate nothing,
rarely leave behind more than a pen—
the inner shell—and an indigestible beak.
The young squid spends its ink on water.
Its three hearts measure out copper blood;
its eyes never close. Look, a thousand
are writhing phosphorescent together,
mating—embracing, competing, refusing, attacking—
and each reads the others' flickering skin,
the colors, stripes, and flashes, like its own mind.
Nothing to mislay or remember.
No wonder they go so fast through the press of the sea.

Stubbornly

for RLB

Pass by the showy rose,
blabbing open,
suckling a shiny beetle;

pass by the changeless diamond
that falls asleep in shadow—

this love is a lichen,

alga and fungus made one fleck,
feeding on what it feeds,

growing slightly faster than stone
into a patch of gray lace,
a double thumbprint,

its bloom distinguishable, with practice,
from its dormant phase,

crocheting its singular habit
over time, a faithful stain
bound to its home,

etching on the unmoved rock
the only rune it knows.

Small Moth

She's slicing ripe white peaches
into the Tony the Tiger bowl
and dropping slivers for the dog
poised vibrating by her foot to stop their fall
when she spots it, camouflaged,
a glimmer and then full-on—
happiness, plashing blunt soft wings
inside her as if it wants
to escape again.

Mawson in a Crevasse

Antarctica, 1913

Through a skin of snow over nothing
he dropped between thin lips of ice
and hangs in a wedge of space,
yanked from the rest of the endless fall
by his fourteen-foot-long harness, lashed
and buckled at its other end
to the half-sledge stuck in broken crust at the brink.
It's shockingly peaceful here, hidden under the wind
that's been the only voice in his ears
since Mertz stopped raving ten days ago—
the wind that can fray rope, unpaint wood,
and scour rust from the chains for the poor old dogs.
Out of the wind on his tether he's turning
in a diminishing spiral,
like milk at the mouth of a drain.

Ninnis went first, and neatly as a posted letter;
if he even had time to cry out the cry went with him
and six of the dogs and most of the food.
In the crevasse down which he disappeared, they saw
one broken dog on a ledge too deep to reach
and ultraviolet walls of ice. No bottom.
The two men left fed dogs to their dogs,
fed them boots and harness, finally
ate dog themselves. His mouth keeps recalling
the feel of stewed paws, which Mertz refused,
favoring liver. Shortly thereafter, their hair and nails
and skin began falling off. Mertz raged and cried,
bit off one finger, spat it out, finally fell silent.
No one else for a hundred miles. With his knife
Mawson hacked a sledge in half and went on.

His spiral motion has decayed to a weave
without discernible pattern. If he climbs out,
he still has most of one hundred miles
to haul the half-sledge and what's left of himself
to the base at Commonwealth Bay. Two hours
he takes every morning just breaking his paltry camp
with black-tipped fingers, watching clumps
of his hair blow away, and a mile or two later
it's night already. He hasn't got far
since he had to bind the soles of his feet back on.
It's good not to feel them squish with each step.
He's lost the cuff of one ear. It's nice not to listen
to his ragged sledge-hauling wheeze. He admires
the cello-toned indigo around him,
like no other color, as one hand gropes for the knife.

While he's been dangling, another South African tribal chief
has called for racial equality,
several more Model Ts have veered from the road,
and Balkan Adrianople lies besieged,
but is anyone in the world closer to death than he?
Yes. Some with diphtheria, cholera, typhoid,
some of the women in difficult labor,
four miners blind in a pocket of gas,
old ones at rest on final pillows,
a black farmer turning to face a sharp noise,
an Irish rebel, a Chinese scholar, a woman near Adrianople
crushed beneath a soldier and biting her hands.
Within a few months King George of Greece, Francisco Madero,
and Mahmud Shevket Pasha will fall to assassins.
Next year, Archduke Ferdinand.

Who is nearer death: Mawson, freezing with his knife,
in tentative swaying motion
like the planchette of a speechless Ouija board?
or the cellist of a quartet in Melbourne?
They're deep into Haydn, the Largo that's played
for funerals, but today for itself, for joy,
and the cellist sways in the dream of needing no more.
He turns the page to the Minuet, with no inkling
that this night, with just such economy of gesture,
having placed the cello, his other body,
beside his bed, he will drop to the floor
and lie without a pulse in a bar of blue light.
And Mawson will have hauled his few pounds of furs and bones
feet-first from the crevasse, and staggered toward food and company,
marriage, two more expeditions, forty-five more years.

But ever after he carried a wedge of space inside
where a pendulum hung, and he was its little weight,
slightly scribbling on the void beneath;
ever after he waited without hurry
for the time when he would find out what it wrote.

The Blessed Elias and the Worm

The Blessed Elias,
who never was made a saint,
within his first year atop the pillar
to which he retired
from the sinful world's ground level
noticed signs of the presence
of the parasite that would be with him
all the rest of his days.
First he rebuked it.
He tried the usual purgatives.
When medicine failed,
he fed it sand and little stones
to teach it the unappetizing nature
of the material sphere.
When its tail, or head,
for who could tell which,
emerged through an abscess,
he wrapped it around
a twig, as advised,
and turned the twig at intervals
to draw out (gently)
its growing length;
they say his self-denial was such
that he'd wind out one new inch in the time
when a man of normal habits
would have twisted out a dozen.
The Blessed Elias reminded the worm
it had chosen a poor host indeed.
He preached it many sermons.
After much prayer and meditation,
often concerning whether

the mortification of his flesh
improved the worm in any way,
the Blessed Elias resolved that this was not
an affliction sent to test him,
but one of God's creatures.
And because in his years on the pillar
he adhered to a vow
of silence on all matters except for faith,
the followers who supplied his meager requirements
were dumbly amazed to hear one day
his voice come down
without its rasp of certainty, saying,
"Perhaps it would like some figs."

Zucchini Shofar

No animals were harmed in the making of this joyful noise:
A thick, twisted stem from the garden
is the wedding couple's ceremonial ram's horn.
Its substance will not survive one thousand years,
nor will the garden, which is today their temple,
nor will their names, nor their union now announced
with ritual blasts upon the zucchini shofar.
Shall we measure blessings by their duration?
Through the narrow organic channel fuzzily come
the prescribed sustained notes, short notes, rests.
All that rhythm requires. Among their talents,
the newlyweds excel at making
and serving mustard-green soup and molasses cookies,
and taking nieces and nephews for walks in the woods.
The gardener dyes eggs with onion skins,
wraps presents, tells stories, finds the best seashells;
his friends adore his paper-cuttings—
"Nothing I do will last," he says.
What is this future approval we think we need;
who made passing time our judge?
Do we want butter that endures for ages,
or butter that melts into homemade cornbread now?
—the note that rings in my deaf ear without ceasing,
or two voices abashed by the vows they undertake?
This moment's chord of earthly commotion
will never be struck exactly so again—
though love does love to repeat its favorite lines.
So let the shofar splutter its slow notes and quick notes,
let the nieces and nephews practice their flutes and trombones,
let living-room pianos invite unwashed hands,
let glasses of different fullness be tapped for their different notes,

let everyone learn how to whistle,
let the girl dawdling home from her trumpet lesson
pause at the half-built house on the corner,
where the newly installed maze of plumbing comes down
to one little pipe whose open end she can reach,
so she takes a deep breath
and makes the whole house sound.

Notes

ELEGY FOR THE QUAGGA (PAGE 7)

The volcanic island of Krakatau, or Krakatoa, erupted August 27, 1883. (The first recorded living thing found later on the still-warm remainder was a spider.) The last known quagga died on August 12 of the same year.

STARLINGS ON THE LINE (PAGE 14)

Both starling releases are historical events. The dots and dashes spell out "please" in Morse code.

BEYOND RUBIES (PAGE 18)

The Tlhorh culture is purely fictional, but the use of "Pig of God" for Jesus in translation is not.

THE MUSEUM OF DAMAGED ART: AUDIO GUIDE (PAGE 19)

Damage to the artworks named is factual. The quotation near the beginning is a paraphrase of a warning posted in the gallery.

THE KINGDOM OF NAB (PAGE 27)

A fictional realm in the neighborhood of the Hittites and Assyrians; its culture and history overlap somewhat with ancient Sumeria's. Apparently it was for some time a city-state like Makris, Ab-insa, Iskot, and Mishgath-Tera, but it eventually conquered some or all of the others.

Least is known about the period called the Early Kingdom, which lasted until about 2100 B.C.E. From the Middle Kingdom, approximately 2100 to 1350 B.C.E., some written records survive. The Late Kingdom, 1350 to 870 B.C.E., has so far yielded the most artifacts and the names of its kings.

The archaeologists and scholars mentioned are likewise fictional except for the great Sir Leonard Woolley ("Destruction") and contemporary physicist John Wheeler ("Flinders"). Two more exceptions:

Adad-nirari I of Assyria and Kadashman-Turgu the Kassite king
("Certainties") were, according to records, actual rulers in 1300 B.C.E.

UNDERGROUND ORCHIDS (PAGE 90)

In southwestern Australia, in desert heat, a type of orchid blossoms
deep underground, and carnivorous plants trap insects for nourishment.

MAWSON IN A CREVASSE (PAGE 106)

Sir Douglas Mawson (1882–1958), Australian hero of the Antarctic,
survived the loss of both comrades, at least one drop into a crevasse,
and vitamin A poisoning to finish one of his journeys over the ice.

The (fictional) string quartet was playing the Largo from Haydn's
Opus 76, No. 5.

About the Author

Sarah Lindsay was born in Cedar Rapids, Iowa, where archaeological digs are few and far between; she graduated from St. Olaf College (having survived four orchestra tours) with a B.A. and a Paracollege major in English and creative writing, and also holds an M.F.A. in creative writing from the University of North Carolina–Greensboro. As either one-third or one-fourth of the personnel at Unicorn Press for several years, she set type, printed pages, and bound books by hand; she also filled orders, swept the floor, and served tea at 4. In her current position as a copy editor at Pace Communications, she has worked on such titles as *Amtrak Express, Southern Bride, IGA Grocergram,* and the inflight magazines for Piedmont, Braniff, USAir, and Delta airlines.

Lindsay has published two chapbooks, *Bodies of Water* (1986) and *Insomniac's Lullaby* (1989), and two books in the Grove Press Poetry Series: *Primate Behavior* (1997), a finalist for the National Book Award, and *Mount Clutter* (2002). Her work has also appeared in *The Atlantic, The Georgia Review, The Kenyon Review, The Paris Review, Parnassus, The Yale Review,* and other magazines.

Copper Canyon Press gratefully acknowledges
Lannan Foundation for supporting the publication and
distribution of exceptional literary works.

LANNAN LITERARY SELECTIONS 2008

Lars Gustafsson, *A Time in Xanadu*

David Huerta, *Before Saying Any of the Great Words:
Selected Poetry*

Sarah Lindsay, *Twigs and Knucklebones*

Valzhyna Mort, *Factory of Tears*

Dennis O'Driscoll, *Reality Check*

LANNAN LITERARY SELECTIONS 2000–2007

Maram al-Massri, *A Red Cherry on a White-tiled Floor: Selected Poems*,
translated by Khaled Mattawa

Marvin Bell, *Rampant*

Hayden Carruth, *Doctor Jazz*

Cyrus Cassells, *More Than Peace and Cypresses*

Madeline DeFrees, *Spectral Waves*

Norman Dubie
The Insomniac Liar of Topo
The Mercy Seat: Collected & New Poems, 1967–2001

Sascha Feinstein, *Misterioso*

James Galvin, *X: Poems*

Jim Harrison, *The Shape of the Journey: New and Collected Poems*

Hồ Xuân Hương, *Spring Essence: The Poetry of Hồ Xuân Hương*,
translated by John Balaban

June Jordan, *Directed by Desire: The Collected Poems of June Jordan*

Maxine Kumin, *Always Beginning: Essays on a Life in Poetry*

Ben Lerner, *The Lichtenberg Figures*

Antonio Machado, *Border of a Dream: Selected Poems*,
translated by Willis Barnstone

W.S. Merwin
  The First Four Books of Poems
  Migration: New & Selected Poems
  Present Company

Taha Muhammad Ali, *So What: New & Selected Poems, 1971–2005,*
  translated by Peter Cole, Yahya Hijazi, and Gabriel Levin

Pablo Neruda
  The Separate Rose, translated by William O'Daly
  Still Another Day, translated by William O'Daly

Cesare Pavese, *Disaffections: Complete Poems 1930–1950,*
  translated by Geoffrey Brock

Antonio Porchia, *Voices,* translated by W.S. Merwin

Kenneth Rexroth, *The Complete Poems of Kenneth Rexroth*

Alberto Ríos
  The Smallest Muscle in the Human Body
  The Theater of Night

Theodore Roethke
  On Poetry & Craft: Selected Prose of Theodore Roethke
  Straw for the Fire: From the Notebooks of Theodore Roethke

Benjamin Alire Sáenz, *Dreaming the End of War*

Rebecca Seiferle, *Wild Tongue*

Ann Stanford, *Holding Our Own: The Selected Poems of Ann Stanford*

Ruth Stone, *In the Next Galaxy*

Joseph Stroud, *Country of Light*

Rabindranath Tagore, *The Lover of God,*
  translated by Tony K. Stewart and Chase Twichell

Reversible Monuments: Contemporary Mexican Poetry, edited by
  Mónica de la Torre and Michael Wiegers

César Vallejo, *The Black Heralds,* translated by Rebecca Seiferle

Eleanor Rand Wilner, *The Girl with Bees in Her Hair*

Christian Wiman, *Ambition and Survival: Becoming a Poet*

C.D. Wright
  One Big Self: An Investigation
  Steal Away: Selected and New Poems

Matthew Zapruder, *The Pajamaist*

The Chinese character for poetry is made up of two parts: "word" and "temple." It also serves as pressmark for Copper Canyon Press.

Since 1972, Copper Canyon Press has fostered the work of emerging, established, and world-renowned poets for an expanding audience. The Press thrives with the generous patronage of readers, writers, booksellers, librarians, teachers, students, and funders—everyone who shares the belief that poetry is vital to language and living.

Major funding has been provided by:

Anonymous (2)

Sarah and Tim Cavanaugh

Beroz Ferrell & The Point, LLC

Lannan Foundation

National Endowment for the Arts

Cynthia Lovelace Sears and Frank Buxton

Washington State Arts Commission

For information and catalogs:

COPPER CANYON PRESS
Post Office Box 271
Port Townsend, Washington 98368
360-385-4925
www.coppercanyonpress.org

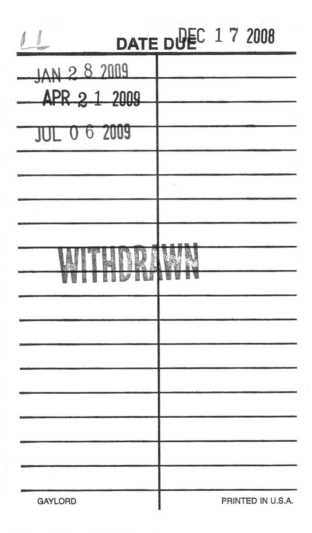

This book is set in Janson Text, a Dutch old-style
designed while Hungarian traveling scholar Miklós Kis
studied in Amsterdam with Dirk Voskens in the 1680s.
Adrian Frutiger and others at Linotype contributed to
this 1985 digital version. The book and part titles are
set in Seria, a font designed by Martin Majoor. Book
design and composition by Valerie Brewster, Scribe
Typography. Printed on archival-quality paper at
McNaughton & Gunn, Inc.